And the Lamb Spoke:
Lessons from the Gospels

Story and Art by
James Thomas Angelidis

jtangelidis.com

To Charlotte!
God Bless!
[signature]

Special thanks to...

Craig Cutler whose idea to write a children's book inspired me to write this book based on our children at Saint Basil Academy in Garrison, NY.

Anna Prokos who helped guide me to make the lessons more child friendly.

Christine Papavasiliou who helped me edit the book into final form.

And the Lamb Spoke
About...

God
Love
Prayer
Giving
Forgiveness
Revenge
Worrying
Judging People
The Golden Rule
Generosity
My Neighbor
Overconfidence
Greatness
Wealth
A Good Life

Basil was a good boy who experienced a lot, more than any child should. His father died and his mother did not have the time or money to care for him. When he was nine, he was sent to a children's home near the mountains of New York. It was beautiful there. Tall trees, mighty mountains and a running river surrounded his new home. There was even a family of deer that pranced around the grounds. But, little could ease the pain of losing his father and mother.

It was autumn and the leaves on the trees were turning colors. Browns, yellows and reds highlighted the trees and above them was the beautiful baby blue sky. It was like a picture perfect painting. There was a cool breeze in the air and the falling leaves gathered below the trees. A few of the children were kicking up the leaves so that they could watch the leaves fall. Suddenly, one of the boys kicked Basil. "You did that on purpose," Basil said. "No, I didn't. You just got in the way," the boy said. "How would you like it if I kicked you?" Basil asked.

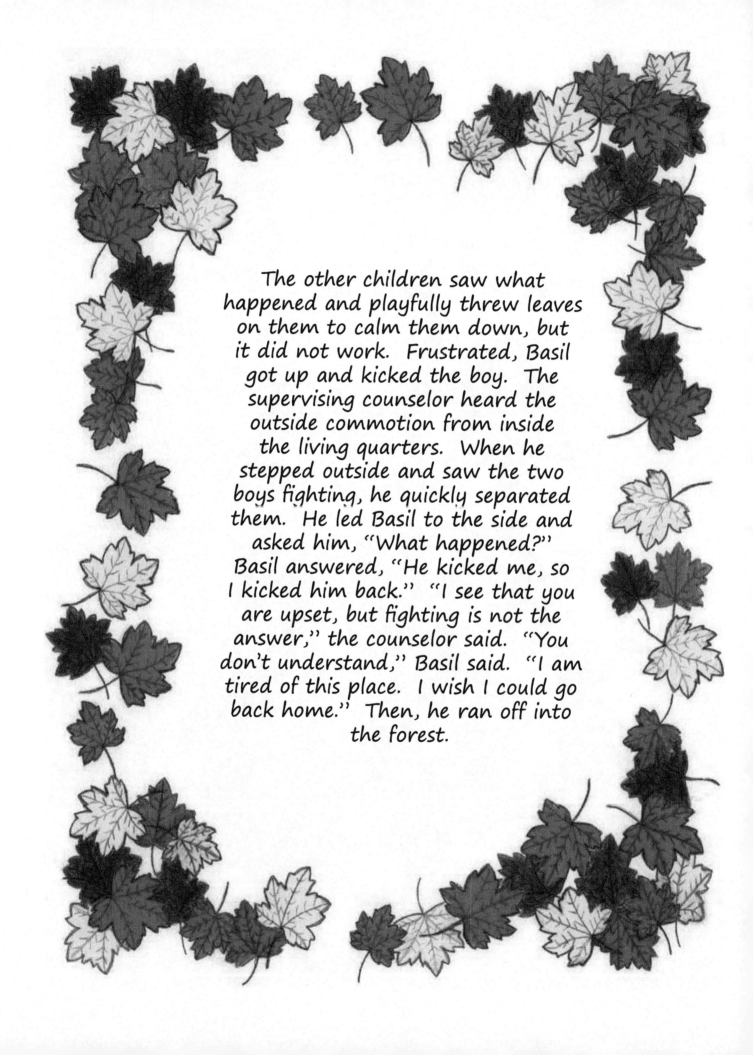

The other children saw what happened and playfully threw leaves on them to calm them down, but it did not work. Frustrated, Basil got up and kicked the boy. The supervising counselor heard the outside commotion from inside the living quarters. When he stepped outside and saw the two boys fighting, he quickly separated them. He led Basil to the side and asked him, "What happened?" Basil answered, "He kicked me, so I kicked him back." "I see that you are upset, but fighting is not the answer," the counselor said. "You don't understand," Basil said. "I am tired of this place. I wish I could go back home." Then, he ran off into the forest.

He ran as fast as he could, but there was nowhere to go. Far from the others and tired, he stopped running in the middle of the forest. As brown, yellow and red leaves danced around him, he dropped to his knees and wept. "Why, God? Why?" he cried out. "Why do others have and I don't? I have no mother to hug me, no father to play ball with me, no home of my own. What do you want from me?"

As he wiped the tears from his face, a calm filled the forest. Above, the sun's rays shone through the trees and warmed him. Then, a lamb appeared. The Lamb's wool was as white as snow. His feet shined like bronze that had been polished. His face was as bright as the midday sun. His eyes blazed like fire. When Basil saw him, he fell down at his feet like a dead man. Then, the Lamb spoke and his voice sounded like a roaring waterfall. He said, "Do not be afraid, my dear child. I heard your cries and have come to your side to comfort you." Basil asked, "What does God want from me?" The Lamb answered, "I am here to tell you."

Basil asked,
"Tell me about God."

The Lamb answered,
"Yes, my dear child...

... God is the Creator who created us
and all things. For those who choose
to listen to God, He becomes their
Heavenly Father and they become
His children and the angels rejoice.
Great rewards in God's Kingdom of
Heaven await those who listen.

At that moment in the forest, the
sun grew bigger, twice as big as it
was just a moment ago. The
sunbeams grew brighter, twice as
bright as they were just a moment
ago. It was as if the sun heard the
Lamb's words and liked what it
heard and got closer to hear more of
what the Lamb had to say.

Basil asked,
"Tell me about love."

The Lamb answered,
"Yes, my dear child...

... God is Love. He wants us to love
Him in return. We show that we
love God by obeying His
commandments. He also wants us
to love our neighbor and even to
love our enemies.

At that moment in the forest, the
big sun grew warmer, twice as
warm as it was just a moment ago.
The bright sunbeams grew more
gentle, twice as gentle as they
were just a moment ago. The sun
seemed to hug Basil as if it knew
that he needed love.

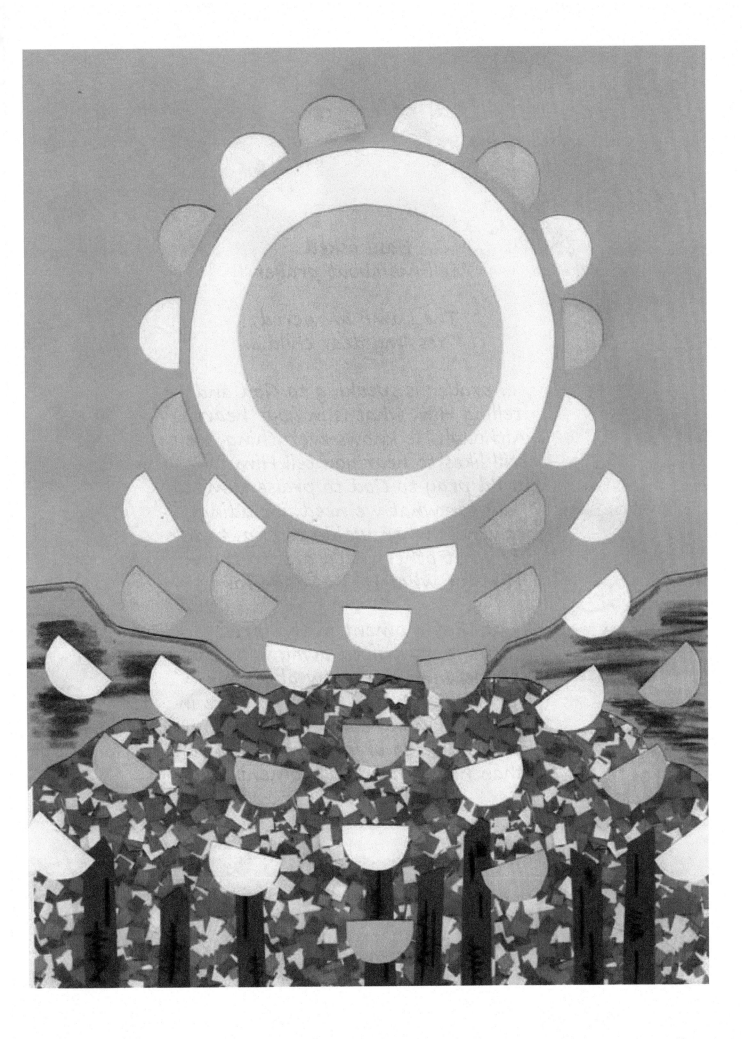

Basil asked,
"Tell me about prayer."

The Lamb answered,
"Yes, my dear child...

... prayer is speaking to God and
telling Him what is in your heart.
Although He knows everything, He
still likes to hear you tell Him. We
should pray to God to praise Him, to
ask for what we need, including
forgiveness when we do wrong, to ask
for what others need and to thank
Him for what He has done for us.

At that moment in the forest,
Basil's fears drifted away with the
gentle wind that blew above him.
The bright sun and fresh air were in
perfect harmony comforting him and
he was able to breathe more deeply
than he could just a moment ago.

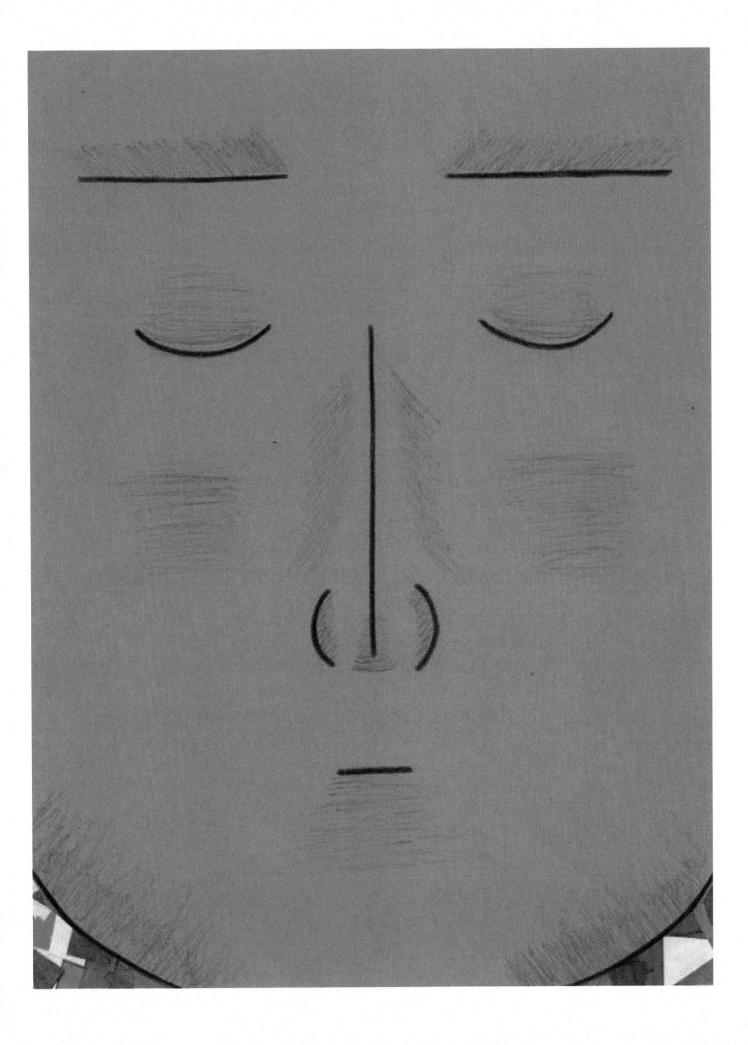

Basil asked,
"Tell me about giving."

The Lamb answered,
"Yes, my dear child...

... when you give something to a
needy person, do not make a big
show of it. Then, it will be a private
matter. And, God, who sees what
you do in private, will reward you.

At that moment in the forest, a
flower blossomed in front of Basil.
Its green bud bloomed into
pretty purple and pink petals. Few
things in nature are as precious and
glorious and he felt blessed to see
the beauty. It was a private gift
from God to Basil.

Basil asked,
"Tell me about forgiveness."

The Lamb answered,
"Yes, my dear child...

... If you forgive people, your
Heavenly Father will also forgive
you; but, if you do not forgive
people, then your Father will also
not forgive you.

At that moment in the forest, a
busy bubbly bumble bee buzzed by
the blooming bud. It liked what
it saw and nestled itself into the
flower. Grateful, it hummed
with happiness.

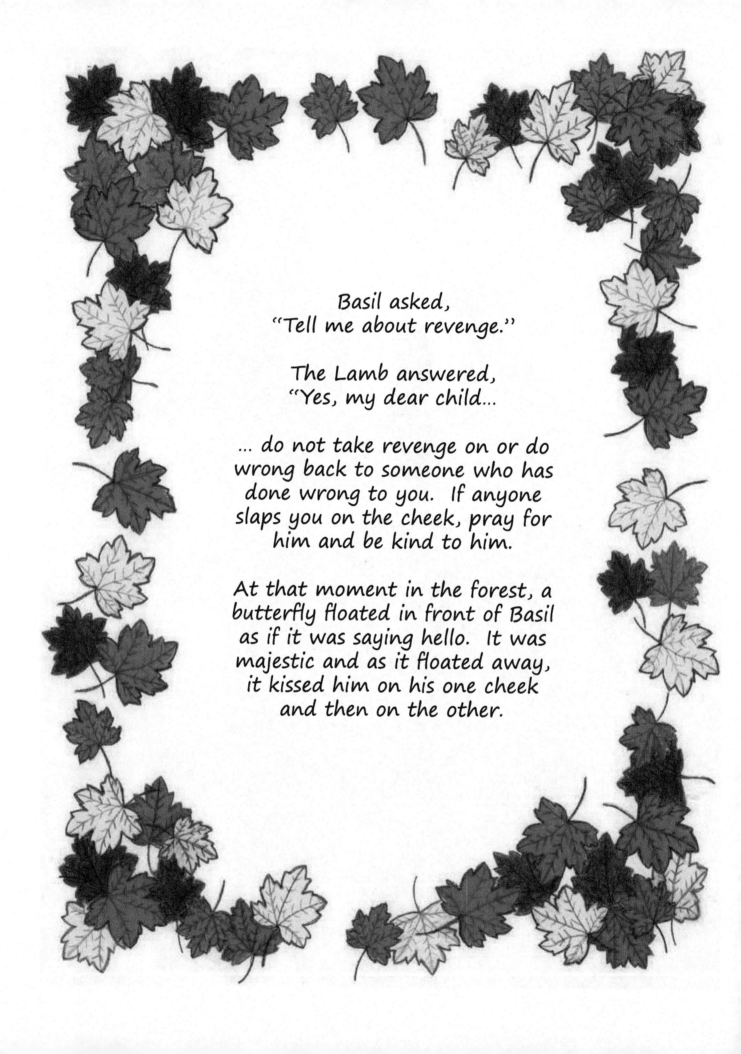

Basil asked,
"Tell me about revenge."

The Lamb answered,
"Yes, my dear child...

... do not take revenge on or do wrong back to someone who has done wrong to you. If anyone slaps you on the cheek, pray for him and be kind to him.

At that moment in the forest, a butterfly floated in front of Basil as if it was saying hello. It was majestic and as it floated away, it kissed him on his one cheek and then on the other.

Basil asked,
"Tell me about worrying."

The Lamb answered,
"Yes, my dear child...

... God knows that you need food,
drink and clothing. Look at the birds:
they do not plant seeds, gather a
harvest and put it in barns; yet, God
takes care of them. Instead, be
concerned, above everything else, with
doing what God says and with what
He asks of you, and He will provide you
with all that you need.

At that moment in the forest, a
family of sparrows flew above
Basil and landed on a high tree branch.
It was a strong branch that carried
them all. It was a perfect spot to
settle themselves and exactly what
they needed to rest their tired wings.

Basil asked,
"Tell me about judging people."

The Lamb answered,
"Yes, my dear child...

... do not judge people or look at other people's wrongdoings or mistakes, so that God will not judge you because God will judge you in the same way you judge people.

At that moment in the forest, a group of dark clouds blocked the shining sun and the air grew thick. Then, it rained with raindrops that were like teardrops.

Basil asked,
"Tell me about the Golden Rule."

The Lamb answered,
"Yes, my dear child...

... the Golden Rule is to treat
others the way you would like
them to treat you.

At that moment in the
forest, the bright yellow sun
broke free from the heavy clouds.
The sun and the misty
atmosphere hugged each other
and created a glowing
rainbow bursting with color.

Basil asked,
"Tell me about generosity."

The Lamb answered,
"Yes, my dear child...

... it does not matter how much money you give. A rich man can give a lot of money and a poor widow can give only a penny. However, the widow would be more generous than the rich man because she gave all she had; while, the rich man gave only what he could spare from his riches.

At that moment in the forest, a snail moseyed his way to a slug that was shivering in the open air. The snail selflessly crawled out of his shell and left it for the slug. He gave all that he could for the sake of the slug.

Basil asked,
"Tell me about my neighbor."

The Lamb answered,
"Yes, my dear child...

... if a man is beaten and robbed
and lying in the street, those who
pass by him and do nothing to
help him are not his neighbor and
are not doing what God would do.
A neighbor is the person who picks
up the man and takes care of him.

At that moment in the
forest, a gazelle fell into a ditch
and a lion appeared. The
gazelle trembled with fear when
he saw the lion. However, out of
compassion, the lion pushed the
gazelle out of the ditch until the
gazelle was free and able to stand
on all four legs.

Basil asked,
"Tell me about being overconfident."

The Lamb answered,
"Yes, my dear child...

... do not be puffed up and think you
are the best because there may be
someone who is greater than you and
you will be embarrassed.

At that moment in the forest, a
curious monkey climbed up a tree and
then stopped because he heard the
Lamb talking. The monkey knew that
to hear a talking lamb was rare. He
was interested in the Lamb's lessons
and listened attentively, as did Basil.

Basil asked,
"Tell me about greatness."

The Lamb answered,
"Yes, my dear child...

... the greatest in God's Kingdom
of Heaven is the one who
humbles himself and becomes
little. And, the leader must be
like a servant.

At that moment in the forest,
an ant gathered all his strength
and lifted up a raspberry and
put it on his back. He carried
it to the anthill where he was
praised and cheered for by his
fellow ants.

Basil asked,
"Tell me about wealth."

The Lamb answered,
"Yes, my dear child...

... true wealth comes from
having God in your life and not
from having many possessions.

At that moment in the forest,
Basil began to pray silently in his
thoughts. He prayed to God to
give him strength and courage to
live life faithfully. He began to
realize that life has meaning and
that God's ways are higher than
our ways.

Basil asked,
"Tell me about how to live
a good life."

The Lamb answered,
"Yes, my dear child...

... a good life is not always easy.
Sometimes, there will be hard
decisions, but if you make the
right choices, God will help you.

At that moment in the forest, a
path of fresh green grass grew
on top of the moist soil and it
led to the children's home.

Basil marveled at the Lamb's answers. He had never heard such beautiful words, so wonderful and full of life. Then, the Lamb said, "Above all, my dear child, know that you are loved. God loves you. God knows you well and even the hairs on your head have all been counted. Trust in Him. Find comfort in Him. He will let you rest in fields of green grass and lead you to quiet pools of fresh water. He will give you new strength. He will guide you in the right paths, as He has promised. Even if you go through the deepest darkness, do not be afraid, for He is with you. His shepherd's rod and staff will protect you. He will prepare a feast for you, where all your enemies can see you; He will welcome you as an honored guest and fill your cup to the top. Know that His goodness and love will be with you all your life; and His house will be your home forever."

Suddenly, the Lamb raised his head and stood at attention. "Did you hear that?" the Lamb asked Basil. "Yes, I did," Basil answered. "It is my Father," the Lamb said, "He is calling me. I must go. But, remember, your Heavenly Father is only a prayer away, and where He is so am I. And, just as you can speak to us in prayer everyday and we listen to you, you can listen to what we have to tell you everyday in the words of the Bible." Then, the Lamb hurried away and Basil walked back to the children's home thinking about what the Lamb taught him.

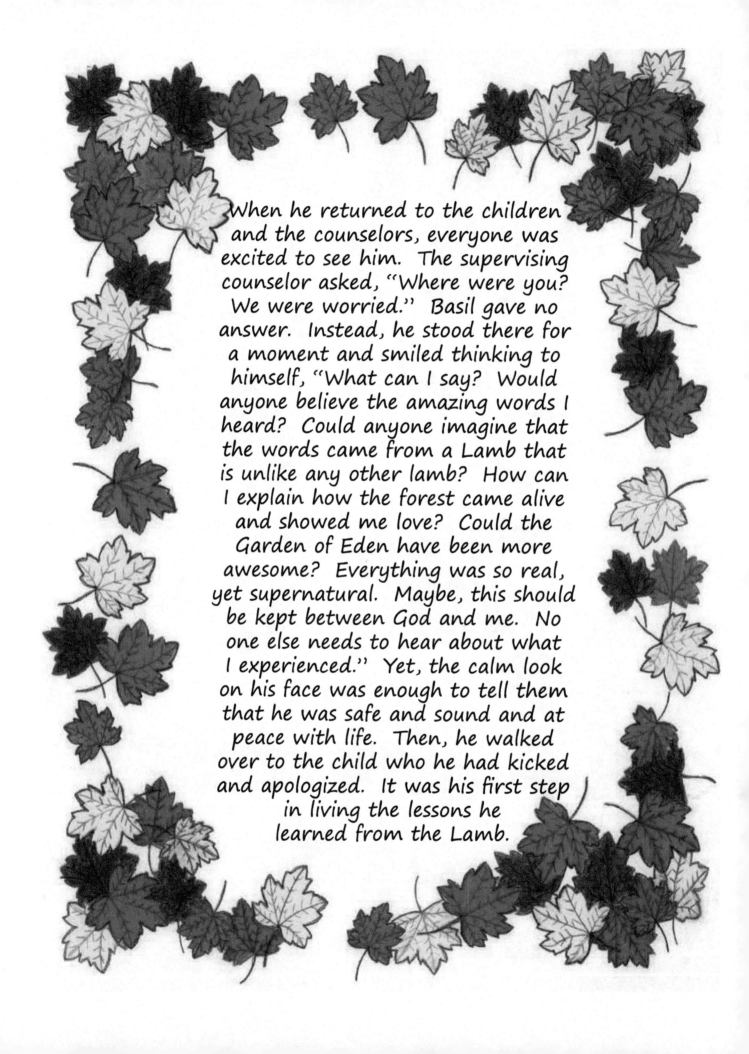

When he returned to the children and the counselors, everyone was excited to see him. The supervising counselor asked, "Where were you? We were worried." Basil gave no answer. Instead, he stood there for a moment and smiled thinking to himself, "What can I say? Would anyone believe the amazing words I heard? Could anyone imagine that the words came from a Lamb that is unlike any other lamb? How can I explain how the forest came alive and showed me love? Could the Garden of Eden have been more awesome? Everything was so real, yet supernatural. Maybe, this should be kept between God and me. No one else needs to hear about what I experienced." Yet, the calm look on his face was enough to tell them that he was safe and sound and at peace with life. Then, he walked over to the child who he had kicked and apologized. It was his first step in living the lessons he learned from the Lamb.

CPSIA information can be obtained
at www.ICGtesting.com
Printed in the USA
BVOW07*0500141117

500097BV00001B/1/P